Decorative
❖ WOOD CRAFTS ❖

Jillybean
Designer, Decorative Painter,
Contributing Writer

Carol L. Spooner
Designer, Decorative Painter,
Technical Consultant

PUBLICATIONS INTERNATIONAL, LTD.

Jillybean (Jill Fitzhenry) is a nationally recognized designer, instructor, publisher, and author. She has served as consultant to major crafts magazines, Binney & Smith, and others in the craft industry. Her latest publications include the "Art Made Easy" series of instructional materials. She is a member of the National Society of Tole and Decorative Painters. Her designs appear on pages 12, 16, 19, 24, 32, 34, 38, 44, 50, 57, and 60.

Carol L. Spooner is a longtime painter who specializes in tole and decorative painting. Her work has been widely published in books and nationally known crafts magazines. She has owned a craft store, taught classes and seminars, and is a member of the National Society of Tole and Decorative Painters. Her designs appear on pages 22, 26, 29, 41, 46, 53, and 62.

Photography: Sacco Productions Limited/Chicago

Photographers: Chris Brooks, Peter Ross

Photo Stylist: Melissa J. Sacco

Model: Karen Blaschek/Royal Model Management

Photo site acknowledgements: Molly and Michael Breem; Laura Barnett Henderson, American Society of Interior Designers; and Teresa and Walter Moeller.

Manufactured in U.S.A.

8 7 6 5 4 3 2 1

ISBN 0-7853-0284-0

❖ Contents ❖

Christmas Sled (page 34)

Mark's Color Box (page 41)

His Keeper and Tray (page 53)

3

❖ Introduction ❖

Decorative painting is an art form that has been handed down from generation to generation. Developed by untrained artists and refined over the years, no artistic talent or drawing skills are necessary. All you need is the desire to create useful and beautiful items.

Once you start painting, you'll be hooked. Let the dishes and dusting wait and indulge yourself. You'll surprise everyone with the decorative pieces you will create. The following pages contain a large variety of styles and finishes from which to choose. Many can be completed in a few hours. Have fun creating all the decoratively painted pieces ahead!

Paints

There are many brands of acrylic paint to choose from; don't be intimated by the number of bottles! Mix and match your favorite colors and brands to paint the projects in this book.

Acrylic paint dries in minutes and cleanup is easy with soap and water. If a project requires a medium that is not acrylic or water based, these will need mineral spirits to clean up. Always check the manufacturer's label before working with a product.

Finishes

To preserve and finish your projects, there are a variety of types and brands of varnishes. Brush on water-base varnishes dry in minutes and clean up with soap and water. Use over any acrylic paints. Don't use over paints or mediums requiring mineral spirits cleanup. Spray varnishes can be used over any type of paint or medium. For projects with a pure white surface, choose a nonyellowing varnish. Varnishes are available in matte, satin, or gloss finishes. Don't be afraid to experiment.

Brushes

Brushes are your most important tool. Foam (sponge) brushes work well to seal, basecoat, and varnish wood, as do large flat brushes. Synthetic brushes work well with acrylic paints, and are reasonably priced. Use a liner brush for thin lines and details. A script brush is needed for extra long lines. Round brushes fill in round areas, stroke work, and broad lines. An angle brush can be used to fill in large areas, float, or side-load color. Small flat brushes are for stroke work and basecoating small areas. A stencil brush and a fabric round scrubber can be used for stencil painting and stippling. The Kemper tool or an old toothbrush can be used to splatter paint.

Painting Supplies

Other supplies you will need include a palette and a water container to rinse brushes. You can use disposable acrylic palette paper, a plastic plate, freezer paper, or foil to put paint on. Paper towels are useful to blot water off brushes. A palette knife can be used to mix color or scoop paint onto the palette. Transparent paper, a pencil, and transfer paper are for tracing designs. A stylus can be used instead of a pencil to trace patterns and can also be used when making dots.

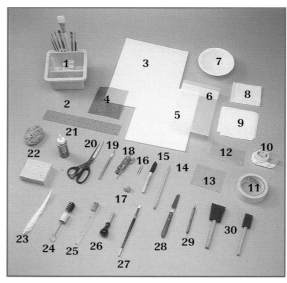

Supplies used in this book: 1) water basin and assorted brushes, 2) ruler, 3) transparent paper, 4) tracing paper, 5) palette paper, 6) heavy plastic (for stencils), 7) plastic bowl, 8) tack cloth, 9) paper towels, 10) transparent tape, 11) masking tape, 12) brown paper (bag), 13) sand paper, 14) pencil, 15) black marker, 16) paper clip, 17) nonabrasive eraser, 18) compass, 19) craft knife, 20) scissors, 21) craft glue, 22) sponges, 23) feather, 24) Kemper tool, 25) old toothbrush, 26) stencil brush, 27) fabric scrubber, 28) palette knife, 29) stylus, 30) foam brushes.

Wood Preparation

Properly preparing your wood piece can make all the difference in the outcome. Having a smooth surface to work on will allow you to complete the project quickly and easily. Once the wood is prepared, you are ready to proceed with a basecoat, stain, or finish, according to the project instructions. Some finishes, such as crackling, will recommend not sealing the wood. Always read instructions completely before starting.

❖ Tips and Alternatives

Wood with knot holes requires a special sealer to prevent sap from later bleeding through the paint. Check the manufacturer's label for proper usage.

1 Choose a clear wood sealer for transparent finishes. Any rough edges should be presanded using #200 sand paper. Wipe wood clean with a tack cloth. Use a foam or large flat brush to apply sealer. Allow sealer to dry completely. You can use a hair dryer to speed drying time, if desired.

2 Once the wood has been sealed and is dry, the grain will raise slightly. Sand with #200 sand paper to smooth surface. Rub your hand across the surface to check for any missed rough spots. Wipe surface with a tack cloth to remove dust particles.

Transferring Designs

You don't have to know anything about drawing to transfer a design. The designs in this book can be transferred directly onto the project surface. Simply follow the instructions for a fast and easy transformation.

Transfer supplies: transparent tracing paper, pencil or fine marker, scissors, tape, transfer paper (carbon or graphite), and stylus.

1 Use transparent tracing paper and place it over the design you want to copy. Trace the design lines with a pencil or fine marker. Trace only the lines you absolutely need to complete the project. The transparent paper allows you to easily position the pattern on the wood project. Cut excess paper to whatever shape or size is easiest to work with. Tape a few edges down to hold the pattern in place.

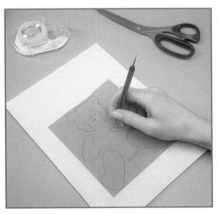

2 Place a piece of transfer paper, carbon side down, between the wood and pattern. Choose a color that will easily show on your project. Use a stylus or pencil to trace over the design lines. Lift a corner of the pattern to make sure the design is transferring properly.

Basic Painting Techniques

Thin Lines

  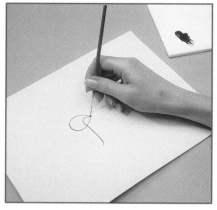

1 Thin paint with 50 percent water for a consistency that flows easily off the brush. It should be about the consistency of ink.

2 Use a liner brush for short lines and tiny details or a script brush for long lines. Dip brush into thinned paint. Wipe excess on palette.

3 Hold brush upright with handle pointing to the ceiling. Use your little finger as a balance when painting. Don't apply pressure for extra thin lines.

Floating Color

This technique is also called side loading. It is used to shade or highlight the edge of an object. Floated color is a gradual blend of color to water.

1 Moisten an angle brush with water. Blot excess water from brush, setting bristles on paper towel until shine of water disappears.

2 Dip the long corner of angle brush into paint. Load paint sparingly. Carefully stroke brush on palette until color blends halfway across the brush. If the paint blends all the way to short side, clean and load again.

3 Hold the brush at a 45 degree angle, and using a light touch, apply color to designated area.

Center Float

For a shadow or highlight in the center of an area, color can be floated with two strokes next to each other. This will make a gradual blend of color to water on both sides of a center area.

1 Load the brush the same as for floated color. Apply one stroke, turn surface half way around and place second stroke next to first. Paint-filled side of the two strokes will lay together.

Double Load Side by Side

This is used to shade or highlight the edge of an object. Two colors are loaded on a brush, one on each side. This can be done with either a round or flat brush.

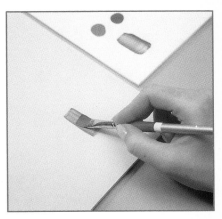

1 Use undiluted paint. Pull the side of the brush through one color of paint. Pull the other side of the brush through another color. Paint should be loaded generously because you will wipe most off during blending on palette.

2 Carefully stroke on palette until colors melt together in the center only. Keep colors side by side while blending. It takes a little practice to keep colors from blending together completely.

3 Keep colors side by side when stroking on the edge of the object you are painting.

Stippling

Create a textured look on an area. Great for foliage, snow, background effects, etc.

1 Use undiluted paint for heavy texture or dilute with 50 to 80 percent water for a soft, faint texture. Dip a fabric scrubber, stencil brush, or old scruffy brush into paint. Dab off excess on paper towel.

2 Hold brush upright and pounce tip of brush repeatedly in area until desired texture is reached. For a light and airy look, don't fill area in completely; allow some of background to show through.

Splattering

Little dots of paint are sprinkled on the surface. Great for creating snow, aged flyspecked look, or just adding fun colors to a finish. Always test splattering on paper first.

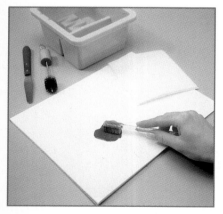 

1 Thin paint with 50 to 80 percent water. Use an old toothbrush and palette knife or a Kemper tool. Dip brush into thinned paint. Lots of paint on the brush will create large dots. As paint runs out, dots become finer.

2 Drag your thumb or palette knife across the top of the toothbrush bristles, causing them to bend. As you release, the bristles will spring forward, splattering the paint onto the surface.

❖ Alternatives

A Kemper tool is like a tiny baby bottle washer with a wire that bends the bristles as you twist the handle. Hold brush over object and twist handle.

Hold a large flat brush vertically in one hand over the surface. Hold the handle of another brush under it horizontally. Tap handle against handle.

Stenciling

This is a method of painting using heavy plastic with shapes cut in it. Simply apply paint inside the shapes with a stencil brush for perfect designs. A sponge or old brush with bristles cut short will also work.

1 Use a precut stencil pattern or make your own by drawing a design on mylar and cutting it out with a craft knife. Tape on surface or spray back of stencil with stencil adhesive.

2 Don't thin the paint. Dip the tip of stencil brush in paint. Blot almost all paint off on paper towel. Too much paint or watery paint can bleed under stencil and cause uneven edges. Practice on paper first.

3 Hold brush in an upright position, pounce repeatedly inside cut out area. Make color heavy on the edges and sparse in the center for a shaded look.

Dots

Perfect round dots can be made with any round implement. The size of the implement determines the size of the dot. You can use the wooden end of a brush, a stylus tip, a pencil tip, or the unused eraser end of a pencil.

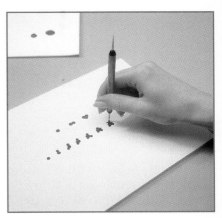

1 Use undiluted paint for thick dots or dilute paint with 50 percent water for smooth dots. Dip the tip into paint and then onto the surface. For uniform dots, you must redip in paint for each dot. For graduated dots, continue dotting with same paint load. Clean tip on paper towel after each group and reload.

2 To create hearts, place two dots of the same size next to each other. Then drag paint from each dot down to meet in bottom of heart. To create teddy bears from dots, follow sequence of dots in picture.

Knob and Pole Printing

This is one of the simplest ways to create decorative printing for the beginner. Letters are made up of thin lines and dots. The letters can have a slight variation in size and still be pleasing to the eye. Always practice on paper first.

1 Print letters lightly on surface with pencil. Line the letters with desired paint color. Use undiluted paint for thick lines or thin with 50 percent water for thin lines.

2 Add a dot on each bend and ends of letters. For O, place dot on top, a bit to the left of center.

Norwegian Rose Marble

Create the look of marble with a little sponging, veining, and blending.

1 Basecoat surface with off white acrylic paint using a soft bristle brush. When dry, brush on a water-base varnish to seal wood. Squeeze small amounts of two colors, such as rose and pink, on palette next to each other. Without mixing, add a drop of extender medium to the top of each—about three parts paint to one part extender. Add the same amount of thickener medium alongside.

2 Wet a natural sponge in clean water and squeeze out all excess water. Pat sponge in both paint and medium a couple times. Blot off excess paint on paper towels.

3 Gently pounce sponge on surface in blotchy, diagonal stripes or drifts, allowing off white to show through. Because surface is sealed, undesirable sponging can be immediately removed with water and paper towels, then reapplied.

4 For veining, set up palette colors, extender, and thickener the same as in Step 2, using medium gray and light gray. Drag the knife edge of a feather through mixture.

5 Apply to surface, outlining the colored blotches by using a jerky, twisted, pulling stroke with the feather. Veins can be softened by dragging a soft dry brush across them if desired. Allow to dry.

6 Splatter with a dark brown color and allow to dry. To finish, protect by spraying with two to three coats of a nonyellowing matte varnish. For a polished marble look, use a gloss varnish.

❖ ❖ ❖

With a few brushes and some bottles of paint, you'll be an expert in no time. So begin with the fun and easy projects in this book and then go on to create your own designs. Happy painting!

❖ Country Apple Basket ❖

A-tisket, a-tasket, a country apple basket! And it's just the right size for carrying everything from apples to craft supplies. This basket can be painted and used the same day with the advantage of fast-drying acrylics.

1 Basket should be smooth and free of dust. Stain basket and lid using 1" flat brush and dark walnut stain. Wipe off excess stain with paper towel. Paint top of handles with red oxide. Sand lid with piece of brown paper bag when dry.

2 Transfer pattern to lid top (see page 5). Use #4 round brush to fill in large apple and edges of other two with red oxide. Fill in lightest areas with unbleached titanium and remaining areas with apricot. Paint seeds burnt umber.

3 Double load #10 flat brush (or #4 round brush) with red oxide and apricot (see pages 6 to 9 for painting techniques). With apricot side out, paint a highlight on edges of apples. Fill in solid highlight with apricot (upper right side of large apple).

4 Double load brush with burnt umber and apricot to fill in stems. Use apricot to fill in top circle of stem.

5 Fill in flower petals with unbleached titanium. Fill in flower center with apricot. Double load brush with apricot and red oxide to shade the center. Use #0 liner to paint thin lines around and inside the petals.

6 Double load brush with hooker's green and unbleached titanium to fill in the leaves and stems.

❖ **Tips and Hints**
Let your imagination go—there are many different ways this basket design can be painted. For a natural look, seal the wood with a clear wood sealer instead of a dark color. Perhaps you may want to use pastel colors. Cut the design into different sections and piece together to fit other wood pieces you'd like to paint.

7 Use end of brush dipped in unbleached titanium to make dots in clusters of three. You may also add dots on basket, staggering groups of dots in middle two rows of weaving (see finished picture). Allow to dry and spray two to three coats of varnish.

❖ Cookie Wagon Express ❖

Yummy, yummy, yummy—fill your tummy with cookies delivered by the cookie wagon express. This delightful candy cane striped wagon looks almost good enough to eat. But use it instead for a unique way to serve your Christmas cookies, candies, or breads.

❖ Paint

DecoArt Americana
Acrylic Paints:
Snow White
Raspberry
Country Red
Blush
Forest Green

❖ Brushes

2" foam
#10 flat
#2 script
#0 liner

❖ Supplies

Wizzer Wagon
Brown paper bag
Tape
Ruler
Pencil with new
eraser
Water base varnish
White wood glue
1 yard of 2³/₄" red
ribbon
Sprig of holly

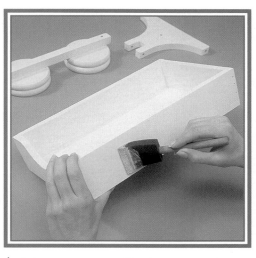

1 Take wheels off of wagon (they will be reassembled at end). Wood should be smooth and free of dust. Apply two coats of snow white with 2" foam brush on entire wagon. Use a piece of brown paper bag to sand when dry.

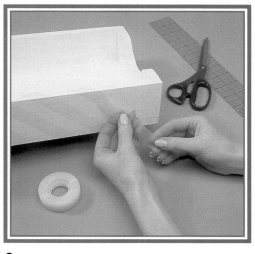

2 Use tape to section off stripes on sides of wagon and handle. Use a ruler to space tape ³/₄" apart. Place pieces of tape at a slant on all sides. For handle, start tape on one end, wrap around in a spiral to other end.

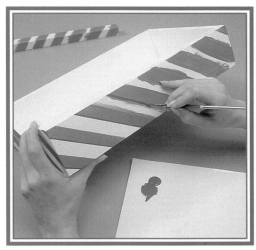

3 Use #10 flat brush to paint raspberry between the tape. Use #2 script brush to add a thin line of country red on left side of each stripe. Allow paint to dry 10 minutes and remove tape.

4 Use the eraser end of a pencil to make the berries in clusters of three on the wheels. Dip the eraser into country red and make five dots around the center hole (dipping into paint for each berry). Add a dot of blush and raspberry next to each red dot.

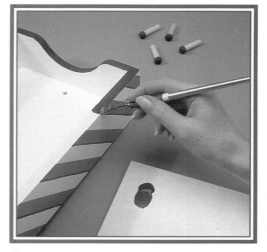

5 Thin forest green with 50% water and use #0 liner brush to make thin lines for the pine needles. Make a line in the center coming out from each berry cluster. Then add shorter thin lines on each side.

6 Paint the trim on the top of the wagon and the pegs for the wheels with forest green using #10 flat brush.

❖ Tips and Hints

Be creative and try cutting contact paper in wavy strips to block out the striped areas instead of tape. Don't use masking tape because it sometimes leaves a residue.

Instead of painting between the stripes with a flat brush, try dabbing paint with a sponge for a textured look.

7 Use your finger to rub country red on the rims of the wheels.

8 Allow paint to dry completely before varnishing. Use 2" foam brush and a water-based varnish to apply two to three coats. Glue wheels and pegs together with white wood glue after varnish is dry. A red ribbon and sprig of holly can be added to the handle.

❖ Hearts and Flowers Checkerboard ❖

Check out this country-style checkerboard. Perfect
checker squares are painted with ease by using tape
to block out areas. What a great centerpiece for a
coffee table or for your game room!

❖ Paint

Fruitwood stain
Liquitex Concentrated
  Artist Colors:
  Baltic Blue
  Red Oxide
  Titanium White
  Hooker's Green
  Yellow Oxide

❖ Brushes

2" foam
#10 flat
#2 script
#4 round

❖ Supplies

Checkerboard and
  checker pieces
Paper towels
Brown paper bag
10" square piece of
  paper
Tracing paper
Transfer paper
Pencil
Tape
Spray varnish

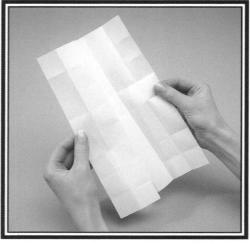

1 Wood should be smooth and free of dust. Brush on acrylic fruitwood stain with 2" foam brush on entire board. Wipe excess off with paper towel. Paint edges with Baltic blue, using #10 flat brush. When dry, sand with a piece of brown paper bag. Paint half of the round checkers with red oxide and the rest with Baltic blue.

2 Make a paper guide that is 10" square. Fold paper in half horizontally. Continue to fold in halves horizontally until you have eight divisions. Open the paper and fold the same way vertically. You now have eight squares in each row.

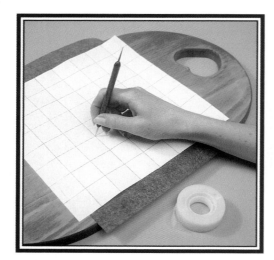

3 Center the paper on the board and use transfer paper to mark the corners of each square. Use tape to block out every other row both horizontally and vertically. Also tape around the outside edge of entire checkered area for sharp outside edges.

4 See pages 6 to 9 for painting techniques. Paint the exposed squares Baltic blue with #10 flat brush. Allow to dry, remove tape, repeat step three, this time taping over the painted rows. Paint the exposed squares Baltic blue. This should complete the checkered pattern. Add a line around the outside edges with red oxide using #2 script brush.

5 Make titanium white dots on the corners of the squares and around the heart cutouts using the tip of a pencil. Dip pencil tip into the paint and onto surface. Dip again in paint for each dot to make them uniform.

6 Transfer design to board on each side, between checkerboard and heart (see page 5). Fill in the design with double loads of color using #4 round brush. Tulip is Baltic blue and titanium white. Paint leaves and stems with hooker's green and titanium white. Large dots are gold oxide and titanium white. Heart is red oxide with gold oxide outline. Allow paint to dry and spray two to three coats of varnish.

❖ **Tips and Hints**

Check out your local stores for precut checkerboard stencil patterns as an option.

You can also use contact paper to block out every other square instead of tape. Simply cut $1\frac{1}{4}$" squares out of the contact paper and place them in every other square.

❖ Perfectly Pretty Plate Shelf ❖

Display your antique or interesting plates on this beautiful wooden shelf. The warm wood grain complements any design applied to the oval. The variety of rub-on transfer designs available will fit any season, room, or decor!

❖ Paint
DecoArt Americana
  Acrylic Paints:
    Buttermilk
    Glorious Gold
Walnut staining glaze
Clear satin sealer

❖ Brushes
1" flat
10/0 liner

❖ Materials
Wooden shelf
Rub-on-transfer
Compass
Pencil
Craft glue
Matte spray varnish

❖ Tips and Hints
Use a different color glaze to complement your own decor or cover the wood grain completely with an acrylic paint.

   When applying a fine border line as we did around the oval, try it on paper first. This will make you more comfortable as you line.

   Before attaching the oval, splatter the shelf with black acrylic paint to give it an older look (also called flyspecking).

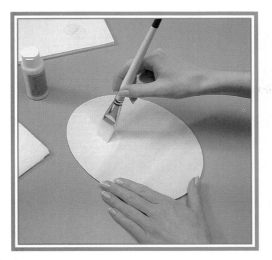

1 Basecoat the oval insert with buttermilk using 1" brush. This may require more than two coats. Allow to dry between each coat.

2 On palette paper, mix equal parts walnut glaze and sealer. Sealer dilutes walnut glaze and seals wood. Test color, then stain shelf and buttons. Do entire sections at one time.

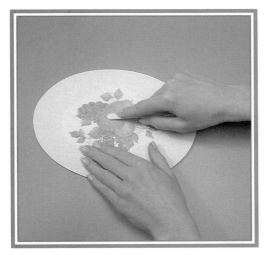

3 Apply the rub-on-transfer; follow manufacturer's directions. Be sure that when you place oval, design is not upside down. Oval is cut to fit one way into hole.

4 With compass, measure ½" from edge of oval and apply a light pencil line. Line with glorious gold using liner brush. Attach buttons and oval with craft glue. Apply matte spray varnish.

❖ Simply Darling Switch Plate ❖

It's so easy to customize light switch plates to
match your decor that you'll want to switch
them all! All it takes to turn ordinary wooden light
covers into decorative wall ornaments is your
leftover wallpaper.

❖ Paint

Liquitex Acrylic Gesso:
    Unbleached Tita-
    nium
DecoArt Americana
    Acrylic Paints:
    Williamsburg Blue
    Snow White

❖ Brushes

1" foam
#10 flat

❖ Supplies

Single wooden switch
    plate
Brown paper bag
Small print wallpaper
    swatch
Scissors
White glue
Paper towels
Large paper clip
High gloss varnish

❖ Tips and Hints

Other papers can be
substituted for
wallpaper, including
wrapping paper or
napkins (see insert).

    High gloss varnish
can be used as glue to
attach the lighter
weight papers to the
switch plate.

    You can use a hair
dryer to speed up
drying time between
coats of paint or
varnish.

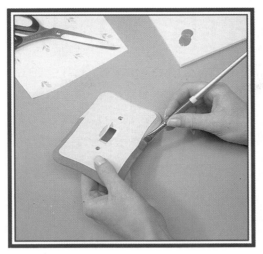

1 Wood should be smooth and free of dust. Basecoat switch plate with unbleached titanium gesso using foam brush. Paint edges with Williamsburg blue using #10 flat brush. Allow to dry and sand with a piece of brown paper bag.

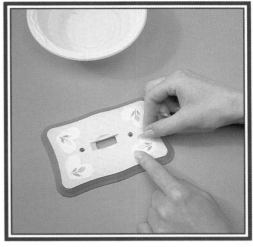

2 Cut out hearts from wallpaper. For prepasted wallpaper, dip cutout in water, wait five minutes, then stick on switch plate. With all other papers, use white glue to adhere. Smooth out all air bubbles with fingers and wipe dry with paper towel.

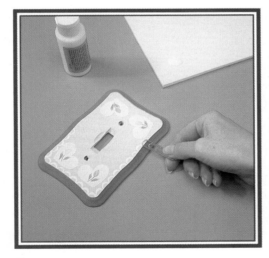

3 Make a lace border by dipping the round end of a paper clip in snow white paint and setting it on the edge (practice on paper before working on switch plate). Add graduated snow white dots using the wooden end of the #10 flat brush. (Dots get smaller as the brush runs out of paint.)

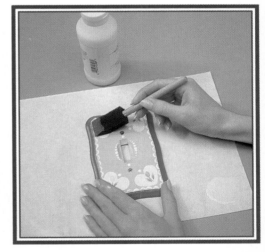

4 Allow paint to dry completely. Use a thick waterbase varnish and apply two to three coats with 1" foam brush. Avoid streaks by brushing on long smooth strokes. Don't stroke over the same area repeatedly.

❖ Spring Norwegian Marble Shelf ❖

Create the beauty of Victoriana with this faux marble
finish and oval of sweet rosebuds. Norwegian rose
marbling is easy and fun; use it to decorate other
areas in your house as well!

1 Basecoat entire shelf with tapioca, let dry. Create the Norwegian rose marble look (see complete steps on pages 10 and 11). Paint oval with tapioca.

2 Stipple (see page 8) background of oval lightly with patchwork green; apply from center of oval to ½" before edge. Center of oval should carry more solid color and fade out.

3 Transfer pattern (see page 5) for outline of rosebuds and leaves only. Using #2 flat brush, paint rosebuds cherokee rose and leaves patchwork green. Apply detail pattern for slit in rosebuds, calyx (leaves around roses), leaf creases, and baby's breath stems.

4 Float shade on rosebuds with rose garden and ³⁄₈" angle brush (see pages 6 to 9 for painting techniques). Float highlight on rosebuds with victorian rose. Line the edge on rosebud slit with victorian rose and liner brush. Float shade on leaves and along crease with thicket, using angle brush.

5 With liner brush, line baby's breath stems with chocolate fudge diluted with water (should be translucent). Dab the baby's breath flower with tapioca. Line the leaves and the calyx with thicket.

6 Using liner brush, line edge of oval with barnwood. When project is dry, finish with matte spray.

❖ **Tips and Hints**
Omit the oval and the rosebuds for a pure marbled look.

Pink can be replaced with a complementary color for your decor.

Try painting on paper and testing colors before applying to project.

❖ Creative Wicker Card Basket ❖

You'll ace your friends when you bring out this wonderful wicker box at your next card party. This creative box can also be used to house other treasures and cherished items. Though it looks complicated, you'll master the technique in no time!

1 Using 1" brush and English mustard, basecoat the entire box (except hinges). Let dry. Apply pattern for twisted reed on top edge (see page 5). Measure all remaining surfaces into ½" × 1" rectangles. Wide reed will run horizontal and the ¹⁄₁₆" narrow reed will be perpendicular.

2 Using 10/0 liner and chocolate fudge, line the rules you have just drawn. Center float (see pages 6 to 9 for painting techniques) a highlight in the middle of each reed using the angle brush and harvest gold.

3 Using angle brush and chocolate fudge, float a shade at the end of each section, both ends of each twisted reed, above and below row of twisted reed, and top and bottom of each narrow reed.

4 Using liner brush and chocolate fudge, apply fine lines on reeds, leaving centers unlined. After project is dry, apply matte spray.

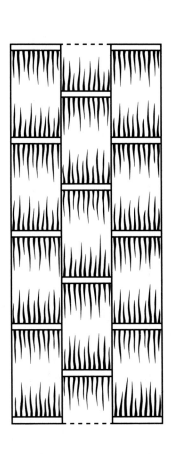

❖ Victorian Sconce ❖

The rosy glow of a candle makes every house cozier!
Create the warmth and charm of a Victorian sconce
shelf in no time at all. Easy to glue on wood
appliqués rubbed with gold add a finishing touch
to this elegant sconce.

❖ Paint
DecoArt Americana
   Acrylic Paints:
   Desert Sand
   Williamsburg Blue
Decorator's Gilt:
   Karat Gold

❖ Brushes
2" foam
Splatter brush or old
   toothbrush
#10 flat

❖ Supplies
Sconce shelf
Brown paper bag
Wood appliqué
Paper towel or soft
   cloth
Wood glue
Spray varnish

❖ Tips and Hints
Wood appliqués with
a traditional sculp-
tured look can be
applied with ease.
These solid wood
shapes can be
custom-stained or
painted to match any
decor.
   Decorator's Gilt
also comes in a
variety of colors and
lends a look of
elegance to your
sconce.

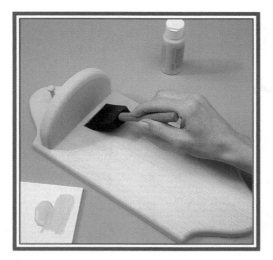

1 Wood should be smooth and free of dust. Brush on desert sand using 2" foam brush. When dry, sand with a piece of brown paper bag.

2 Splatter Williamsburg blue on sconce (see page 8). Allow to dry. Use Williamsburg blue and #10 flat brush to paint the wood appliqué front. Allow to dry.

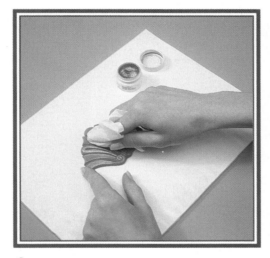

3 Use your finger wrapped in a soft cloth or paper towel to rub gilt on edges of sconce and top of wood appliqué. Rub only the top ridges of wood appliqué, allowing blue to show through the creases.

4 Use wood glue to attach wood appliqué to top of sconce. Weigh down with a heavy object while drying. Allow to dry 12 hours before finishing. Spray two to three coats of varnish on sconce.

❖ Christmas Sled ❖

Slide into the Christmas season with a starlit tree and presents. Ready-to-use stencil patterns are a fun and easy way to paint this decorative sled. Just set the pattern down and paint!

❖ Paint

Liquitex Acrylic Gesso:
  Unbleached Tita-
    nium
DecoArt Americana
  Acrylic Paints:
  Country Red
  Forest Green
  Burnt Umber
  Blush
  Raspberry
  Tangerine
Snow Tex

❖ Brushes

2" foam
#10 flat
Small stencil
#10 fabric scrubber
#2 script

❖ Supplies

Sled
Brown paper bag
Christmas stencil
Paper towels
Tape or stencil
  adhesive spray
Pencil
Spray varnish

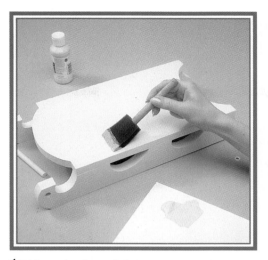

1 Wood should be smooth and free of dust. Basecoat entire sled with unbleached titanium gesso using 2" foam brush. When dry, sand with a piece of brown paper bag.

2 Paint edges of sled with country red using #10 flat brush. Cut out stencil using pattern and heavy plastic instead of buying it, if desired.

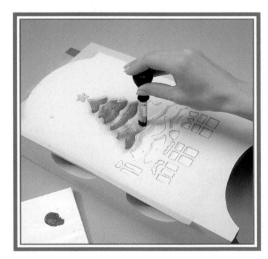

3 To stencil, dip tip of stencil brush in desired color, dab almost all paint off on paper towel, and pounce gently inside stencil areas. Using less paint takes longer but prevents color from seeping under stencil edge. Apply colors heavier on edges and less in center areas for slight shading. Stencil tree forest green; trunk burnt umber; packages combinations of country red, blush, and raspberry; and stars tangerine.

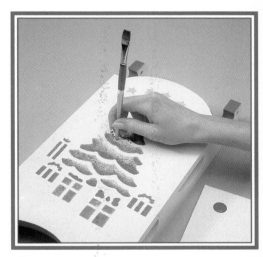

4 Make strands of graduated dots through the tree with country red using the wooden end of the #10 flat brush (see page 9).

35

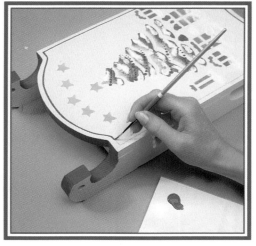

Tips and Hints

Many different precut stencil designs are available at your local arts and crafts stores. Choose your favorite designs and use any brand of acrylic paint. You can also use colored pencils to fill in stencils instead of paints.

5 Use #10 fabric scrubber brush to apply thick layers of Snow Tex on the tree and under presents.

6 Lightly pencil in a stripe about an inch in from each edge. Paint thin country red stripes around the edges of the top and sides of the sled using #2 script brush. Thin paint with 50% water for thin lines. Paint sides of top of sled (above runners) with flat brush and country red.

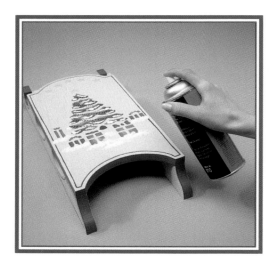

7 Allow to dry completely before varnishing. Spray with two to three coats of varnish.

❖ Country Red Apple Inn Birdhouse ❖

The birds will be waiting in line to move into
this adorable birdhouse. What a fun conversation
piece this is. Display it on your kitchen counter,
mantle, in a grapevine wreath, or hang it outside to
delight the birds!

❖ Paint
Liquitex Concentrated
  Artist Colors:
  Lacquer Red
  Hooker's Green
  Unbleached Tita-
    nium
  Apricot
  Titanium White

❖ Brushes
2" sponge
#10 flat
#4 round
#6 round fabric
  scrubber
#0 liner (optional)

❖ Materials
Apple birdhouse
Tracing paper
Transfer paper
Pencil
Permanent black
  marker (thick line)
Spray varnish

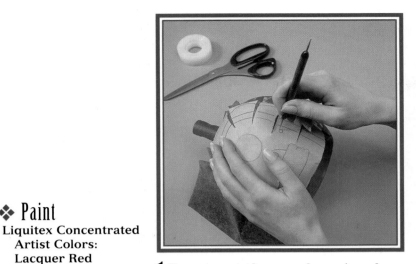

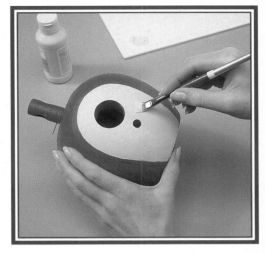

1 Basecoat the apple using lacquer red and 2" sponge brush. When dry, transfer the pattern onto the apple (see page 5). Paint leaf hooker's green.

2 Use #10 flat brush to paint the door and worm hole with unbleached titanium.

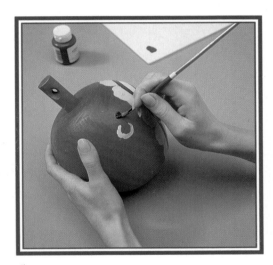

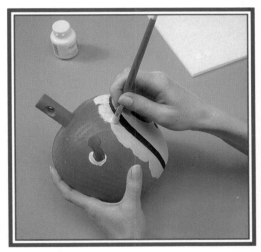

3 With #4 round brush, paint stones around door apricot. Paint worm, door trim, and hole hooker's green. Paint sign titanium white.

4 Stipple titanium white on each stone using #6 round scrubber (see page 8). Don't fill in with solid color.

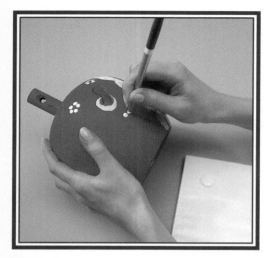
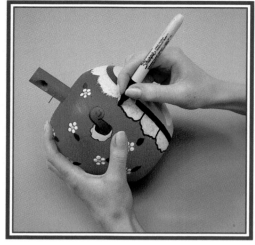

5 Make titanium white dot flowers randomly all over the apple using the wooden end of the # 10 flat brush. Redip the brush for each dot, making five white dots in a circle. Add an apricot dot in the center of each flower. The leaves should be painted with hooker's green using #4 round brush.

6 Use a black marker (or black paint and liner brush) to outline worm, stones, door sign, door trim, and words on sign. Attach leaf. When dry, spray two to three coats of varnish.

❖ **Tips and Hints**
Think of all the different color combinations you could use to paint this cute birdhouse—perhaps country blue with pink and cream accents. Or try one of the other styles of painting described in this book, such as a pickled finish or stenciling.

HOME TWEET HOME

❖ Mark's Color Box ❖

This fun box will delight the kid you love! Make it a project to do with the child or use it to surprise her or him on a special occasion. This is the ideal storage box for crayons, and it can stand up to the rough and tumble treatment kids will give it.

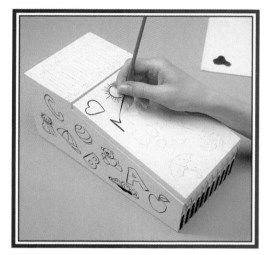

(see page 10)

❖ Paints
DecoArt Americana
  Acrylic Paint:
    Buttermilk
FolkArt Pure
  Pigments:
    Burnt Umber
    Ultramarine Blue
    Ebony Black
    Sap Green
    Pure Orange
    Dioxazine Purple
    Yellow Medium
    Rose Crimson
    Phthalo Green
    Red Light

❖ Brushes
1" flat
10/0 liner
#2 flat

❖ Supplies
Wooden box
Tracing paper
Transfer paper
Pencil
Permanent black
  marker
Colored markers
Matte spray varnish

❖ Tips and Hints
Have the child do all the printing, first with a light pencil, then again with the marker. This is a real treasure to keep and can store any special items a child wants to save.

1 Basecoat entire box with buttermilk and 1" brush. Let dry. Apply pattern for all objects (repeat side pattern). Apply child's name and Color Box in knob-and-pole style (see page 10). Line everything with ebony black and 10/0 liner brush (dilute to ink consistency with water) or line with permanent black marker.

2 Have child color objects all over the box using markers. Option: Using transparent colors, wash each object with slight color (dilute paint with water) and #2 flat brush. Bold black lines will show through. See project for suggested colors.

3 When dry, finish with matte spray.

❖ Handy Heart Hanger ❖

Here's a hang up that will be a pleasure. Fun, fast,
and easy is the best way to describe this coat hanger.
Just cut out some heart shapes, sponge over them
with paint, and splatter some colors here and there.

❖ Paint

Liquitex Acrylic Gesso:
   Unbleached Tita-
   nium
DecoArt Americana
   Acrylic Prints:
   Raspberry
   Blush
   Country Red
   Forest Green

❖ Brushes

2" foam
Splatter brush or old
   toothbrush

❖ Supplies

Wooden coat hanger
Brown paper bag
Contact paper
Scissors
Pencil
Sponge
Spray varnish

❖ Tips and Hints

An endless variety of
shapes can be found
in your own home.
Simply trace around
any object you'd like
to place on the
hanger.
   You can also use
your finger to dab
paint around the
edges of cutouts
instead of a sponge.

1 Wood should be smooth and free of dust. Paint the wood with one coat of unbleached tita-nium gesso using foam brush. When dry, sand with a piece of brown paper bag.

2 Trace heart pattern on contact paper and cut out. Remove backing and place on the hang-er. Using raspberry, dab color around edges of shapes with sponge. (Dab some paint off be-fore applying.)

3 Splatter blush, country red, and forest green on the hanger (see page 8).

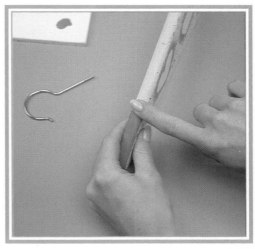

4 Allow paint to dry and remove contact paper shapes. Use your finger to apply raspberry to the edges of the hanger. Spray two to three coats of varnish on the hanger when paint is dry.

❖ Bettina Keepsake Book Box ❖

When a precious baby is born, it's tempting to save everything. This durable keepsake box will hold treasured memories forever. This is an original and thoughtful gift to give or make for your own special bundle!

❖ Paint
DecoArt Americana
  Acrylic Paints:
  Buttermilk
  Raw Sienna
  Baby Pink
  Glorious Gold
  Ebony Black

❖ Brushes
1" flat
Medium stencil or old
  brush
10/0 liner

❖ Supplies
Book box
Stencil
Ruler
Pencil
Stylus
2 craft hinges, 1" each
Matte spray varnish

❖ Optional Supplies
Blank envelopes
Blank note cards and
  envelopes
5" × 7" wooden photo
  frame

1 Basecoat entire box with buttermilk using 1" brush. Let dry. Tape teddy bear stencil to cover of box and stencil with raw sienna paint; stencil heart with baby pink (see page 9). If any bleeding has occurred, carefully clean edges by reapplying buttermilk with a brush.

3 Preprint letters lightly on wood surface with pencil. When placement is correct, line letters with ebony black. Using stylus, dot each bend and end of every letter with ebony black.

2 For trim, start 1" from outside edge, marking sides first. Beginning 2½" from top, mark every ½" and stop at 9" mark. Mark across bottom (1" from bottom edge) every ½" beginning at 1½" mark and stopping at 6½" mark. Border alternates teddy bear, dot, heart, dot, and repeat. Begin top of each row with a teddy. Practice on paper first. Plain dots are glorious gold. Hearts and teddies are pink. (See page 9 for how to make teddies and hearts.) Remember: For dots to be consistent, dip brush into paint for each dot applied.

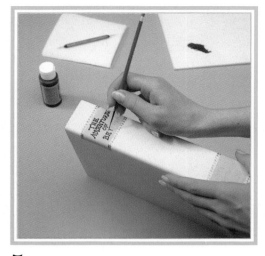

4 Place two rectangles, each 1½" tall, on binder. One is 1" from top and the other is 1" from bottom. Paint these with pink. Line top and bottom of rectangles with gold, then dot outside edges.

5 Pencil words in rectangles. Line with ebony black, diluting with water, and dot with brush handle or stylus. Dot teddy bear's eyes on front with ebony black.

❖ **Tips and Hints**

This box can be customized by changing paint colors from pink to blue.

Line the box with fabric.

Add accessories such as note cards, first tooth envelope, first haircut envelope, and a picture frame by applying the same border across these items.

6 After paint is dry, attach lid with hinges. Apply matte spray.

❖ Pickled Candle Box ❖

You won't get yourself in a pickle with this Victorian style candle box—you'll impress everyone! This fast method for creating an old-fashioned pickled finish is easy and fun. Use the box to store candles for that romantic candlelit dinner.

❖ Paint

White stain and sealer
DecoArt Americana
   Acrylic Paints:
   Williamsburg Blue
   Mauve
   Glorious Gold

❖ Brushes

2" foam
1" foam
#1 liner

❖ Supplies

Candle box
Brown paper bag
Plastic cups or bowls
Tracing paper
Transfer paper
Pencil
Matte spray varnish

❖ Tips and Hints

Pickling is fun to do
in any color combina-
tions that you choose.
Use any brand of
acrylic paint to mix
into white stain.

  Add a twist by
dabbing the color mix
on with a natural
sponge.

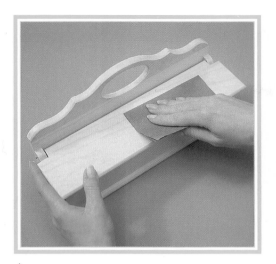

1 Wood should be smooth and free of dust. Apply one coat of white stain using 2" foam brush. Wood grain will show through. Allow to dry and sand with a piece of brown paper bag.

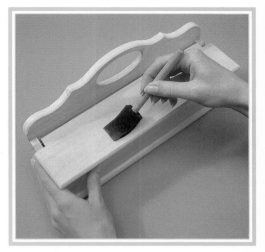

2 Mix ten parts white stain with one part Williamsburg blue in a plastic cup. Use 1" foam brush to apply mix sparingly all over box. Allow to dry and repeat with a mix of ten parts white stain and one part mauve. These multiple transparent colors give the look of pickling.

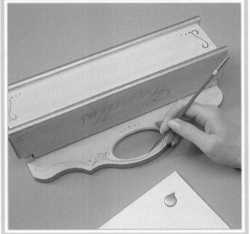
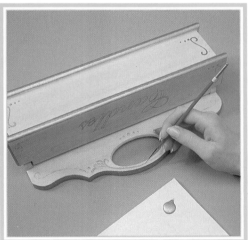

3 When paint is dry, transfer on design (see page 5). Paint with glorious gold using #1 liner. Use your finger to apply glorious gold to edges of box.

4 Allow to dry and spray with a nonyellowing varnish.

❖ Note:
Turn transparent
paper over and center
oval to trace other
side of design.

❖ His Keeper and Tray ❖

Brighten your den with these peaceful geese! The box has three compartments under the narrow lid and one large compartment under the large lid. The oval plaque is a unique tray to set keys and change on, preserving your wood furniture.

❖ Paint

**DecoArt Americana
Acrylic Paints:**
Snow White
Ebony Black
Sable Brown
Colonial Green
Country Blue
Avocado Green
Dark Chocolate
Walnut staining glaze

❖ Brushes

#2 flat
½" flat
10/0 liner
1" flat
Splatter brush or old
   toothbrush

❖ Supplies

Transfer paper
Tracing paper
Pencil
Coarse sandpaper
Tack cloth
Matte spray varnish
¾" felt stick-on tabs

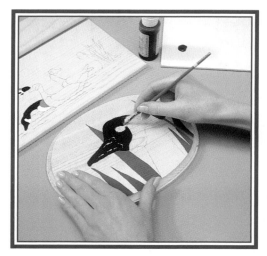

1 Trace and apply pattern to both lids and tray (see page 5 for transferring instructions). Base-coat in designated colors (see finished design for color placement) to areas using #2 flat for small areas and ½" for larger.

2 Using 10/0 liner and ebony black (dilute with water to ink consistency), line entire pattern, creating a coloring book look. Let all paint dry completely.

3 Using coarse sandpaper, sand the painted area. This will scratch some paint off to let wood show through. Use tack cloth to remove dust.

4 Apply walnut staining glaze to entire box and tray with 1" flat brush. Use long strokes over lid for even distribution. Let dry completely.

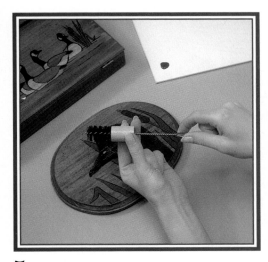

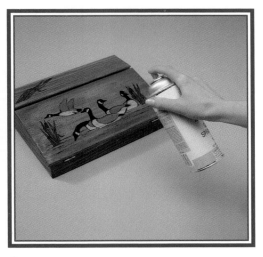

5 Attach lids to box with hinges. Splatter box and tray with ebony black, diluted with water, using splatter brush or old toothbrush.

6 When dry, apply matte spray to finished pieces. When spray is dry, attach the felt protective tabs to bottom of tray and box.

❖ **Tips and Hints**

Small lid can easily be personalized with simple knob-and-pole printing.

You can match your furniture colors by using other available colors of staining glaze.

The tray can be used instead as a plaque to decorate your wall.

❖ Homey Tissue House ❖

This adorable little house tissue box is nothing to sneeze at! You can create a new home to store your tissues. Decorate this little house with faux finishes, decals, and easy-to-paint patterns.

❖ Paint

Liquitex Acrylic Gesso:
  Unbleached Titanium
DecoArt Americana
  Acrylic Paints:
  Williamsburg Blue
  Glorious Gold
  Buttermilk
Rose Pompeii faux
  finishing glaze

❖ Brushes

2" foam
1" foam
Splatter brush or old
  toothbrush
#4 round
#1 liner

❖ Supplies

House tissue box
Brown paper bag
Natural sponge
Paper towels
Gold flower decals
Spray varnish

1 Wood should be smooth and free of dust. Basecoat the entire box with unbleached titanium gesso using a 2" foam brush. Paint the edges of the roof with Williamsburg blue using your finger. When dry, sand with a piece of brown paper bag.

2 Use a natural sponge to dab Williamsburg blue on the roof. Apply color sparingly for a light, airy, textured look.

3 Liberally brush rose Pompeii glaze on sides of house using a 1" foam brush. Immediately blot with a crumpled up paper towel. Complete one side of the house at a time. Allow to dry 12 hours.

4 Apply flower decals according to directions. Soak in water, remove from paper, set on bottom edge of house, and smooth out air bubbles. Allow to dry before continuing.

5 Splatter entire house with glorious gold (see page 8). Paint chimney Williamsburg blue. Use your finger to dab glorious gold on the edges of the roof and chimney (allow some blue to show through).

5 Splatter entire house with glorious gold (see page 8). Paint chimney Williamsburg blue. Use your finger to dab glorious gold on the edges of the roof and chimney (allow some blue to show through).

6 Apply pattern to front and side of house. Basecoat window and door in buttermilk using #4 round brush. Paint door trim, door knob, shutters, and window panes in Williamsburg blue. Paint buttermilk hearts on shutters. Paint glorious gold curve on shutters, window frame, and door frame using #1 liner brush. Allow to dry 12 hours before varnishing. Spray two to three coats of varnish.

❖ **Tips and Hints**
Many different decals are available, from teddy bears to butterflies. Be creative with the flower decals by cutting them into smaller sections. Apply them randomly all over the house.

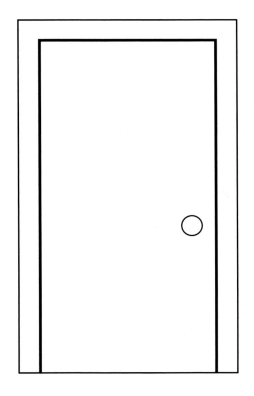

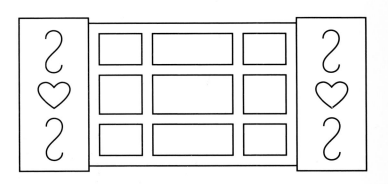

❖ Aged-to-Perfection Mirror ❖

Mirror, mirror on the wall—aged to perfection in no time at all. Watch the cracks appear in the paint right before your eyes. You can make the mirror look like it came from grandma's attic!

❖ Paint
DecoArt Americana
  Acrylic Paints:
  Antique White
  Glorious Gold
  Burnt Umber
  Black

❖ Brushes
1" or 2" stiff bristle or
  2" foam
#10 flat
Splatter brush or old
  toothbrush

❖ Supplies
Wooden mirror
Crackle medium
Decal
Spray varnish

❖ Tips and Hints
Use any good quality
acrylic paint with the
crackle medium for a
wonderful aged look.

Patterns can be
traced on the crackle
medium using a wax
graphite paper,
rather than using a
decal.

Do not paint
multiple layers of
paint—it will cover up
the crackle effect.

1 Wood should be smooth and free of dust. Do not seal the wood. Use the foam or stiff bristle brush to apply a thin coat of crackle medium to front and edges of mirror. (You can stain or paint mirror back.) Allow to dry.

2 Use the foam brush to apply long, even strokes of antique white. Do not stroke over cracks once they begin to appear. Apply glorious gold with #10 flat brush on the outside and inside edges of frame. Apply a thin coat, allowing the darkness of the crackle medium to show through. The gold will not crackle but will appear old.

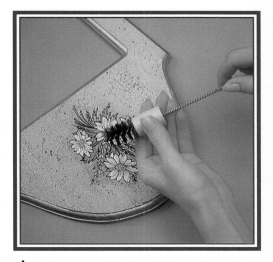

3 Apply decal by first dipping in warm water for 30 seconds, then slide decal off paper. Lay on mirror, smoothing out air bubbles gently. (Be sure not to rub too hard or you may remove crackle.)

4 Splatter with both burnt umber and black (see page 8). Allow to dry 12 hours, then spray two to three coats of varnish.

❖ Ribbons and Lace Clock ❖

This lovely clock, with its Victorian lace and ribbon look, is a sure thing to keep you on schedule. Its simplicity is just enough to add that special accent to any room.

❖ Paint

Accent Country
   Colors Spray:
     Light Stoneware
       Blue, matte
Accent Acrylic Paints:
   Off White
   Stoneware Blue
   Light Stoneware
     Blue
   Roseberry
   Victorian Mauve
   Light Pink Blossom

❖ Brushes

1" flat
10/0 liner
#2 flat

❖ Supplies

Solid wood clock
4" decorative doily
Tracing paper
Transfer paper
Pencil
Matte spray varnish

1 Basecoat entire clock with off white and 1" brush. Let dry. Moisten doily with water and lay in position on the clock face. The center of doily should be over center hole of clock.

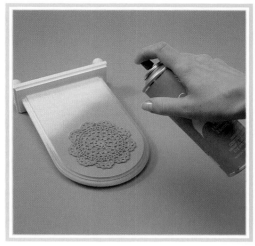

2 After doily has dried on clock face, spray with light stoneware blue. Let paint dry, then remove doily. Paint base and edges of clock with off white. Paint balls and small routered edge with stoneware blue and #2 flat brush.

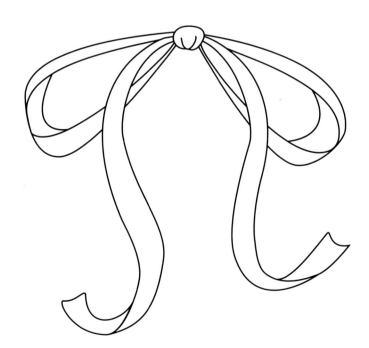

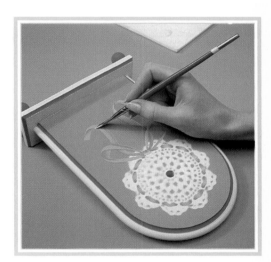

3 Transfer bow pattern onto surface (see page 5). Paint all ribbon victorian mauve and paint ribbon through every other hole on doily. Shade with roseberry. Highlight with mix of victorian mauve and light pink blossom (see pages 6 and 7 for painting techniques). Spray with matte spray to finish. Attach clock.

❖ Materials List ❖

Most products are available in craft stores nationwide.

❖ Wood Suppliers:

Cabin Craft Midwest
P.O. Box 270
Nevada, IA 50201
Hearts and Flowers Checkerboard, Checkers, Pickled Candle Box, Christmas Sled, Simply Darling Switch Plate, Aged-to-Perfection Mirror, Homey Tissue House, Handy Heart Hanger

Cabin Craft Southwest
1500 Westpark Way
Euless, TX 76040
Bettina Keepsake Book Box

Hunt Woodcraft Products, Inc.
P.O. Box 805
Lapeer, MI 48446
Perfectly Pretty Plate Shelf, His Keeper

Piedmont Sales
Loveland, CO 80539
His Tray

Treasures
P.O. Box 9
Huntsville, OH 43324
Mark's Color Box

Viking Woodcrafts, Inc.
1317 8th St. SE
Waseca, MN 56093
Country Apple Basket, Country Red Apple Inn Birdhouse

Walnut Hollow Woodcraft Products
Highway 23 North Rte. 1
Dodgeville, WI 53533
Ribbons and Lace Clock, Spring Norwegian Marble Shelf, Creative Wicker Card Basket, Cookie Wagon Express, Victorian Sconce

❖ Paint, Media, and Other Supplies:

Accent Products Division
Lake Zurich, IL 60047
Accent Country Colors®, Staining Glazes, Sealers

Binney & Smith, Inc.
Easton, PA 18044-0431
Liquitex® Concentrated Artist Colors, Brushes, High Gloss Varnish, Soluvar® Matte Picture Varnish

DecoArt Acrylic Paint
Stanford, Kentucky 40484
DecoArt™ Acrylic Snow-Tex

Decoral, Inc.
Farmingdale, NY 11735
Handpainted Decals

Herr's & Bernat
Danville, IL 61834-0630
Acclaim palette and tracing paper, Gloss Spray Finish

J.W. etc. Quality Products
Simi Valley, CA 93065
Right-Step™ Clear Varnish, White Lightning Stain Sealer

Kemper Tools, Inc.
Chino, CA 91710
Splatter Brush, Double-Ball Stylus

Loew Cornell
Teaneck, NJ 07666-2490
Loew Cornell® Brushes

Plaid Enterprises
Norcross, GA 30091
FolkArt®, Pure Pigment®, Simply Stencils®, Brush Basin®

Robert Simmons Brushes
New York, New York 10011
Tolemaster Brushes

Wang's International
Memphis, TN 38118
Painted Impressions Rub-On-Transfers®

❖ Color Chart ❖

This color chart is for suggested replacements only. Colors will not match exactly, and different batches of a company's colors may vary. We do not guarantee that the colors will match identically.

DecoArt®	FolkArt®	Accent®	Liquitex®
Snow White	Wicker White	Real White	Titanium White
Buttermilk	Tapioca	Off White	
Antique White	Butter Pecan	Wicker	Unbleached Titanium
Ebony Black	Licorice	Real Black	Ivory Black
Dark Chocolate	Chocolate Fudge	Burnt Umber	
Raw Sienna			Raw Siena
Sable Brown			Taupe
Burnt Umber	Coffee Bean	Sweet Chocolate	Burnt Umber
Desert Sand	Vanilla Cream		
	Gray Flannel		
	Platinum Gray		
	Barnwood		
Avocado	Ripe Avocado or Patchwork Green	Chateau Moss	Olive
Colonial Green	Poetry Green	Village Green	
Forest Green			
Evergreen	Thicket	Pine Needle Green	
Leaf Green	Holiday Green	Green Meadow	Hooker's Green
	Amish Blue	Lt. Stoneware Blue	
Blue Haze	Township Blue	Chesapeake Blue	Baltic Blue
Baby Blue			
Country Blue			
Williamsburg Blue		Stoneware Blue	French Gray/Blue
Baby Pink			
Raspberry	Rose Garden		Dk. Victorian Rose
Country Red	Red Clay	Pueblo Red	
Mauve	Cherokee Rose	Roseberry	Venetian Rose
Blush			
Tangerine			
Dusty Rose	Berries N' Cream	Victorian Mauve	
Flesh	Victorian Rose	Lt. Pink Blossom	Pale Portrait Pink
Brandy Wine	Apple Spice		Red Oxide
Berry Red	Christmas Red	Pure Red	Lacquer Red
Medium Flesh		Peaches N' Cream	Apricot
			Yellow Oxide
Glorious Gold	Pure Gold	King's Gold	Metallic Gold

There is no comparable product for Plaid Pure Pigment colors.